PUDDINGS & DESSERTS

Traditional recipes for tempting puddings and desserts

CONTENTS

Guide to symbols

The recipes in this book are accompanied by symbols that alert you to important information.

 Tells you how many people the recipe serves, or how much is produced.

 Indicates how much time you will need to prepare and cook a dish. Next to this symbol you will also find out if additional time is required for such things as marinating, standing, proving, or cooling. You need to read the recipe to find out exactly how much extra time is needed.

 Alerts you to what has to be done before you can begin to cook the recipe, or to parts of the recipe that take a long time to complete.

 Denotes that special equipment is required. Where possible, alternatives are given.

 Accompanies freezing information.

Techniques

Make ice cream

Ice cream can be easily made by hand, or with a machine for a finer texture.

By hand

1 Split 2 vanilla pods, and scrape out and reserve the seeds. Add the pods to a pan with 500ml (16fl oz) double cream, and bring to boil. Add 75g (2½oz) golden caster sugar, and stir until dissolved.

2 In a bowl, whisk 4 egg yolks until well combined, then strain the warm cream mixture into the eggs, stirring all the time. Add the reserved vanilla seeds, and stir.

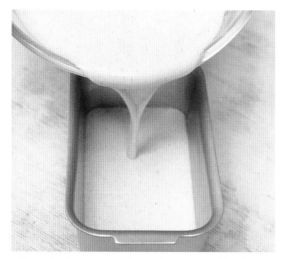

3 Pour the ice cream mixture into a metal loaf tin or plastic tub. Leave to cool completely.

4 Once cool, put into the freezer. When frozen, double-wrap with cling film and freeze for up to 3 months.

With an ice cream machine

1 Prepare a custard (see steps 1 and 2, opposite) and cool in a bowl set over a separate bowl of ice. Stir the mixture continuously to prevent a skin forming on the surface.

2 Pour the custard mixture into an ice cream machine. Continue churning or processing until thick and smooth, then place in a container and freeze until firm.

Make granita

Combine sugar, fruit juice, and water (or red or white wine) to make a syrup that can be frozen to create a light and refreshing dessert.

1 Slowly bring the ingredients to boil, reduce heat, and simmer for 2–3 minutes, stirring. Cool, pour into a shallow baking tray, and freeze. When half-frozen, use a fork to break up the chunks.

2 Break up the crystals once or twice more until evenly frozen. Remove from the freezer 5–10 minutes before serving, to thaw slightly. Scrape up the frozen granita and serve in pre-chilled glasses.

Make fruit sorbet

Lighter than ice cream and a perfect palate cleanser.
You can use any berries.

1 Combine 75g (2½ oz) of sugar in a pan with 60ml (2fl oz) water. Simmer gently for 5–10 minutes, until the sugar has dissolved, and the mixture has thickened.

2 Put 1kg (2¼lb) of strawberries in a food processor, and whiz until puréed. (Alternatively, pass them through a sieve to remove the seeds.) Pour the syrup mixture into the puréed strawberries and stir.

3 Pour the mixture into a freezerproof container – the shallower the better (it will freeze quicker). Leave to cool completely, then put into the freezer.

4 When frozen, remove and stir well to break up any ice crystals, then put back into the freezer. Sorbet is best eaten within a few days, as the fresh fruit taste starts to fade after a while.

Make lacy crêpes

Making these crêpes involves two essentials – the right temperature and the perfect batter. See p10 for ingredient quantities.

1 Heat a little clarified butter in a crêpe pan and pour off any excess. Holding the pan at an angle, pour in a little of the batter.

2 Tilt and swirl the pan as you pour in more batter to thinly and evenly coat the base of the pan.

3 When the crêpe has cooked to a pale gold colour underneath, use a long spatula to loosen and flip the crêpe back into the pan.

4 Cook until the second side is golden. Place on baking parchment with a layer between each finished crêpe. Continue cooking the rest of the batter.

Make French meringue

This meringue will be caramelized and crunchy on the outside and soft and yielding inside.

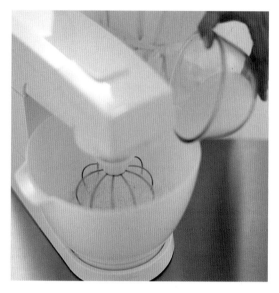

1 In a large mixing bowl, whisk together 3 egg whites, 85g (3 oz) caster sugar, and the seeds from 1 vanilla pod at a moderate speed.

2 Continue whisking until the mixture becomes smooth, shiny, and firm.

3 Using a rubber spatula, gradually fold a further 85g (3 oz) sugar into the egg mixture, taking care not to lose any of the volume.

4 Shape the meringue (see opposite), then bake it so that the centre is just golden. Turn off the oven. Prop the oven door open and leave to dry for at least 8 hours, or overnight.

Shape meringue

A pastry bag can be used to shape meringue or to apply it as a topping to a tart. Prepare a baking tray with parchment before shaping.

For discs or layers, using a pastry bag with a star tip, pipe the meringue in a spiral beginning in the centre and moving outward. Bake for 1 hour 20 minutes, then let dry.

For shells, using a pastry bag with a round tip, pipe the meringue into equal-sized globes and bake for 1 hour 10 minutes, then let dry.

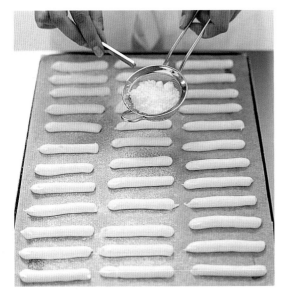

For fingers, using a pastry bag with a round tip, pipe the meringue into thin, even sticks, and dust them with icing sugar. Bake for 30–35 minutes, then let dry.

To cover a tart, using a pastry bag with a star tip, pipe the meringue over top of the tart in attractive peaks. Dust with icing sugar and place under a hot grill for a few minutes, or until golden brown.

Lemon and sugar crêpes

A favourite treat for breakfast, lunch, or tea, these simple pancakes are a family favourite.

INGREDIENTS
115g (4 oz) plain flour
¼ tsp salt
1 egg
300ml (10fl oz) milk
about 3 tbsp vegetable oil, for frying
lemon wedges and caster sugar, to serve

METHOD
1 Sift the flour and salt into a large bowl and make a well in the centre. Add the egg and milk and whisk together, gradually drawing in flour from the sides, to make a smooth, thin batter. Slowly add the remaining milk, beating until smooth. Leave to stand for 10 minutes.
2 Preheat the oven to its lowest setting. Heat the crêpe pan over a high heat until hot. Pour in enough vegetable oil to coat the bottom of the pan, swirl around, then pour off the excess.
3 Ladle 3 tablespoons of the batter into the centre of the pan and tilt so that it covers the base thinly. Cook the crêpe for 1–2 minutes, or until small bubbles appear. Slide a palette knife underneath and flip over, then continue cooking for 30 seconds, or until golden. (See p7 for step-by-step technique.)
4 Remove and keep warm in the oven. Repeat until all the batter has been used.
5 Serve hot, sprinkled with sugar and lemon juice.

serves 4

prep 5 mins, plus standing • cook 10 mins

18cm (7in) crêpe pan

freeze, interleaved with greaseproof paper, for up to 3 months

Cherry clafoutis

This French favourite can be enjoyed warm or at room temperature.

INGREDIENTS
750g (1lb 10 oz) cherries
3 tbsp kirsch
75g (2½ oz) caster sugar
butter, for greasing
4 large eggs
1 vanilla pod, split in half lengthways
100g (3½ oz) plain flour, sifted
300ml (10fl oz) milk
pinch of salt

METHOD
1 Toss the cherries with the kirsch and 2 tablespoons of the sugar in a medium-sized bowl, and leave to stand for 30 minutes.
2 Meanwhile, preheat the oven to 200°C (400°F/Gas 6). Butter the flan tin, and set aside.
3 Strain the liquid from the cherries and beat it with the eggs, the seeds from the vanilla pod, and the remaining sugar. Slowly beat in the flour, then add the milk and salt, and mix to make a smooth batter.
4 Arrange the cherries in the flan tin, then pour the batter over. Place in the oven and bake for 35–45 minutes, or until the top is browned and the centre is firm to the touch.
5 Dust with sifted icing sugar and allow to cool on a wire rack. Serve warm or at room temperature. This is delicious served with thick cream, crème fraîche, or vanilla ice cream.

serves 6

prep 12 mins,
plus standing
• cook 35–45 mins

25cm (10in)
flan tin

Pineapple and syrup upside-down pudding

This sunshine-coloured pudding is baked "upside-down" so the pineapples are on top when it is turned out.

INGREDIENTS

2–3 tbsp golden syrup
400ml can pineapple rings, drained
150g (5½ oz) butter
125g (4½ oz) golden caster sugar
2 eggs
175g (6 oz) self-raising flour, sifted
1–2 tbsp milk

METHOD

1 Preheat the oven to 180°C (350°F/Gas 4). Grease the ovenproof dish. Drizzle in the golden syrup to cover the base, then top with the pineapple rings, and put to one side.

2 Place the butter and sugar in a bowl, then whisk with an electric hand whisk until pale and creamy. Mix in the eggs, one at a time, adding a little of the flour after each one. Fold in the remaining flour, then add the milk a little at a time until the mixture drops easily off the beaters. Pour the mixture over the pineapples and bake in the oven for 40–50 minutes, or until golden brown and springy to the touch. Serve hot from the oven.

serves 4–6

prep 10 mins,
• cook 50 mins

1.2-litre (2-pint) ovenproof dish • electric hand whisk or mixer

freeze the pudding in its dish, wrapped in cling film, for up to 3 months

Banoffee pie

Always a hit, this dessert's name derives from its delicious filling of fresh bananas and toffee sauce.

INGREDIENTS
20cm ready-made tart case
200g (7 oz) ready-made thick caramel
  sauce (such as Dulce de leche)
2–3 ripe bananas
300ml (10fl oz) double cream
  or whipping cream
25g (scant 1 oz) dark chocolate

METHOD
1 Place the tart case on a serving plate. Spoon in the caramel sauce and spread evenly. Slice the bananas and scatter over the top.
2 Put the cream in a bowl and whisk with an electric hand whisk until soft peaks form, then spoon over the bananas. Grate the chocolate over the top and serve.

serves 8

prep 15 mins

electric
hand whisk

Classic pavlova

This classic meringue dessert is named after Russian ballerina Anna Pavlova, but credit for inventing it is claimed by both Australia and New Zealand.

INGREDIENTS

6 egg whites, at room temperature
pinch of salt
350g (12 oz) caster sugar
2 tsp cornflour
1 tsp vinegar
300ml (10fl oz) double cream
strawberries, kiwi fruit, and passion
   fruit, to decorate

METHOD

1 Preheat the oven to 180°C (350°F/Gas 4). Line a baking tray with greaseproof paper. Put the egg whites in a large, clean, grease-free bowl with a pinch of salt. Whisk until stiff, then start whisking in the sugar 1 tablespoon at a time, whisking well after each addition. Continue whisking until the egg whites are stiff and glossy, then whisk in the cornflour and vinegar.

2 Spoon the meringue on to the baking tray and spread to form a 20cm (8in) circle. Bake for 5 minutes, then reduce the oven to 140°C (275°F/Gas 1) and cook for a further 1 hour and 15 minutes, or until the outside is crisp. Allow it to cool completely before transferring to a serving plate.

3 Whip the cream until it holds its shape, then spoon it on to the meringue base. Decorate with the fruit and serve.

serves 6

prep 15 mins,
plus cooling
• cook 1 hr 20 mins

Raspberry crème brûlée

Fresh raspberries make this classic French dessert extra special.

INGREDIENTS
200g (7 oz) fresh raspberries
4 large egg yolks
8 tbsp golden caster sugar
560ml (18fl oz) double cream
1 tsp pure vanilla extract

METHOD
1 Divide the raspberries among the ramekins. Put the egg yolks and 2 tablespoons of the sugar in a large bowl and whisk with an electric hand whisk until the mixture begins to thicken and becomes pale and creamy.
2 Heat the cream gently in a pan for 5 minutes. Do not let it boil. Remove from the heat, stir in the pure vanilla extract, and allow to cool for 5 minutes.
3 Slowly add the warm cream to the egg mixture a little at a time, whisking constantly. When it's all in, pour the mixture back into the pan, and cook over a low heat for a couple of minutes, stirring all the time with a wooden spoon until thick. Do not allow to boil. Pour the custard into the ramekins and allow to cool completely. Transfer to the refrigerator to set for a couple of hours or overnight.
4 When ready to serve, sprinkle the tops of the custards evenly with the remaining sugar and place under a hot grill until the sugar bubbles and turns golden brown. Alternatively, use a cook's blowtorch, making sweeping movements with the flame until the sugar starts to caramelize. Allow the topping to harden for 20 minutes before serving.

serves 6

prep 10 mins,
plus chilling
• cook 45 mins

chill for at least
2 hrs, or overnight
if possible

6 ramekins
• electric
hand whisk

Mini summer puddings

Summer pudding is usually one big dessert, but this recipe gives guests an individual pudding all to themselves.

INGREDIENTS
about 9 slices white bread, crusts
   removed
700g (1lb 9oz) mixed summer berries
   and currants
75g (2½ oz) caster sugar, or to taste
icing sugar, to dust (optional)

METHOD
1 Line the pudding basins with the bread, tearing the slices into pieces to fit. Remember to reserve some bread to fit the tops after the fruit has been added. Make sure the basins are well lined – any gaps will cause the puddings to collapse when turned out.

2 Put the fruit in a pan with caster sugar and 250ml (9fl oz) water. Bring to the boil, stirring until the sugar dissolves. Simmer gently for 5 minutes, or until the berries start to soften and release their juices. Test for sweetness and add a little more sugar if needed. Spoon some of the juice into the basins so the bread starts to soak it up. Divide the berries among the basins, pushing them down to pack in as many as possible and letting the bread absorb the juice – no white bread should show when the puddings are turned out. Packing in as many fruits as possible will prevent the puddings collapsing. Cover the berry filling with the remaining bread, and then spoon over the last of the juice until no white bread is visible.

3 Cover each basin tightly with cling film and leave to chill in the refrigerator for at least 2 hours. To serve, turn out onto individual serving plates. Dust with icing sugar before serving, if you like.

serves 6

prep 30 mins,
plus chilling

chill for at least
2 hrs, or overnight
if possible

6 x 200ml (7fl oz)
pudding basins

freeze the puddings in
their basins, covered
with cling film, for up
to 2 months

Sticky toffee and banana pudding

A lovely winter pudding that is as fast to prepare as it is sure to be consumed.

INGREDIENTS

115g (4 oz) butter
115g (4 oz) light muscovado sugar
200ml (7fl oz) double cream
6 tbsp maple syrup
225g (8 oz) ginger cake, sliced
2 large bananas
60g (2 oz) pecan nuts, chopped

METHOD

1 Preheat the oven to 190°C (375°F/Gas 5). Place the butter, sugar, cream, and maple syrup in a small pan and heat gently, stirring constantly, until smooth.
2 Lightly grease the ovenproof dish. Arrange the cake and bananas in the dish, pour the sauce over, and scatter the pecans over the top. Bake for 10 minutes, or until the toffee sauce is bubbling.

serves 6

prep 5 mins,
• cook 10 mins

20 x 30cm (8 x 12in)
ovenproof dish

Chocolate mousse

For the ultimate chocolate sensation, this is best made with dark chocolate containing at least 70 per cent cocoa solids.

INGREDIENTS

100g (3½ oz) 70 per cent dark chocolate,
  broken up
1 tbsp milk
2 eggs, separated
35g (1¼ oz) caster sugar
150ml (5fl oz) double cream
dark chocolate, grated or curled to serve
  (optional)

METHOD

1 Place the chocolate and milk in a heatproof bowl over a pan of simmering water. When the chocolate has melted, stir until combined, remove from the heat, and allow to cool slightly.

2 Place the egg yolks and sugar in a large bowl and whisk until thick and creamy. Then whisk in the chocolate mixture.

3 Whip the cream in a bowl until stiff. Gently fold in the chocolate mixture until combined, taking care not to overmix. Whisk the egg whites until stiff, and gently fold into the chocolate mixture.

4 Spoon into individual dishes and refrigerate for at least 2 hours. If you like the mousse soft, take it out of the refrigerator and let it warm to room temperature before serving. Decorate with grated chocolate or chocolate curls.

serves 6

prep 20 mins,
plus chilling
• cook 20 mins

Lemon and praline meringue

Impressive to serve at dinner parties,
but quite easy to make.

INGREDIENTS

3 egg whites
pinch of salt
175g (6 oz) caster sugar

For the praline

60g (2 oz) granulated sugar
60g (2 oz) whole blanched almonds
pinch of cream of tartar

For the filling

150ml (5fl oz) double cream
3 tbsp lemon curd
85g (3 oz) dark chocolate

METHOD

1 Preheat the oven to 130°C (250°F/Gas ½) and line a large baking tray with
   greaseproof paper.
2 Whisk the egg whites with the salt, until stiff but not dry. Add 2 tablespoons of sugar,
   and whisk again until smooth and shiny. Continue to add sugar, 1 tablespoon at a time,
   whisking well after each addition. Spoon into a piping bag with a star nozzle attached,
   and pipe six 10cm (4in) diameter circles on to the baking-parchment lined tray
   (see p11). Bake for 1 hour 30 minutes, or until crisp.
3 Meanwhile, make the praline. Oil a baking tray and put the sugar, almonds, and cream
   of tartar into a small, heavy saucepan. Set the pan over a gentle heat and stir until the
   sugar dissolves. Boil until the syrup turns golden, then pour out on to the greased
   baking tray. Leave until completely cold, then coarsely chop.
4 When ready to serve, whip the cream until just holding a trail, and fold in the lemon
   curd. Melt the chocolate in a heatproof bowl over a pan of gently simmering water.
   Don't allow the bowl to touch the water. Spread each meringue with a little chocolate.
   Allow to set, then pile the lemon curd cream on top, sprinkle with praline, and serve.

serves 6

prep 35 mins
• cook 1 hr
30 mins

piping bag
and star nozzle

Red fruit terrine

All the flavours of summer are wrapped up in this stunning red berry terrine.

INGREDIENTS

75g (2½ oz) caster sugar
90ml (3fl oz) elderflower cordial
juice of 1 lemon
2 tbsp powdered gelatine
225g (8 oz) raspberries

115g (4 oz) redcurrants
140g (5 oz) blueberries
225g (8 oz) ripe strawberries, quartered
extra fruit, to decorate

METHOD

1 Place the sugar in a saucepan with 450ml (15fl oz) water. Heat gently until the sugar has dissolved. Bring to the boil and boil the sugar mixture for 1–2 minutes. Cool slightly then stir in the elderflower cordial and the lemon juice.

2 Place 4 tablespoons of warm water into a small bowl and sprinkle the gelatine over. Leave to soak for 2 minutes. Place the bowl in a pan of hot water and stir until the gelatine has dissolved. Stir into the syrup.

3 Place the non-stick loaf tin into a roasting tin. Pack crushed ice halfway up the sides of the roasting tin and pour a little water over the ice. Scatter the raspberries into the bottom of the loaf tin and pour over enough elderflower syrup to cover. Allow to set.

4 Scatter the redcurrants and blueberries over the rasbesrry layer and pour over enough elderflower syrup to cover. Allow to set. Finally, scatter the strawberries over and pour in the remaining syrup. Transfer the roasting tin to the fridge and chill for at least 3 hours, or preferably overnight, until set.

5 To turn out, dip the loaf tin into hot water for few seconds and invert onto a plate. Carefully remove the loaf tin. Decorate with extra fruit.

serves 4–6

prep 45 mins, plus chilling • cook 5 mins

chill for at least 3 hrs, or overnight if possible

900g (2lb) non-stick loaf tin

Quick tiramisu

This luscious Italian dessert gets its name, which means "pick-me-up", from the espresso coffee.

INGREDIENTS
120ml (4fl oz) cold espresso coffee
75ml (2½fl oz) coffee-flavoured liqueur
350g (12 oz) mascarpone cheese
3 tbsp caster sugar
350ml (12fl oz) double cream
14 sponge fingers
cocoa powder, to decorate
coarsely grated dark chocolate,
  to decorate

METHOD
1 Mix the coffee and liqueur together in a shallow, wide serving bowl and set aside.
2 Put the mascarpone cheese and sugar in a bowl, and beat for a minute or two, until the sugar dissolves. Whip the cream in another bowl until it holds its shape, then fold it into the mascarpone mixture. Put a couple of spoonfuls of the mascarpone mixture in the bottom of a serving dish.
3 Dip and turn 1 sponge finger in the coffee mixture until just soaked, then place it on top of the mascarpone in the dish; repeat with 6 more sponge fingers, placing them side by side in the dish. Cover with half the remaining mascarpone mixture, then soak and layer the remaining sponge fingers. Top with the remaining mascarpone and smooth the surface. Cover the dish with cling film and refrigerate for at least 4 hours.
4 Sprinkle the top with cocoa powder and grated chocolate just before serving.

serves 4

**prep 20 mins,
plus cooling
and chilling**

**chill for at least
4 hrs**

Caramel oranges

The sweet caramel sauce is a perfect match for the sliced fruit.

INGREDIENTS
4 oranges
225g (8 oz) caster sugar
crème fraîche, to serve

METHOD
1 Remove the zest from 1 of the oranges using a potato peeler; take care not to include any of the white pith. Cut the zest into very thin slivers and set aside.
2 Cut the zest and pith away from the other oranges. Slice the oranges, arranging them back into the shape of a whole orange, then place the slices in a mixing bowl.
3 Place the sugar in a saucepan with 150ml (5fl oz) water. Heat gently until the sugar dissolves. Increase the heat and boil for 8–10 minutes, or until the mixture turns a golden brown colour. As it boils, dip a pastry brush in cold water and brush around the inside of the pan to stop sugar crystals from forming. Slowly add another 150ml (5fl oz) of water to the caramel. Be careful (it will splutter a little), and stir to combine.
4 Stir in the reserved orange zest slivers and cook, stirring for 4–5 minutes, or until softened. Pour the syrup over the oranges and leave to stand overnight.
5 Serve each orange fanned out on a serving plate with a spoonful of crème fraîche. Drizzle with the caramel syrup.

serves 4

prep 10 mins, plus standing • cook 15 mins

prepare the day before serving to infuse the flavours

Zesty lemon granita

Italians eat this as a refreshing sweet treat on a hot day, but it also makes a delicious dessert after a rich meal.

INGREDIENTS
6 lemons
115g (4 oz) caster sugar
twists of lemon zest, to decorate

METHOD

1 Set the freezer to its coldest setting and place freezerproof serving bowls or glasses in the freezer. Using a cannelle knife or lemon zester with a v-shaped cutter, thinly pare the zest from 4 of the lemons, and set aside, then grate the zest from the remaining 2 lemons, and set aside, separately.

2 Dissolve the sugar in 250ml (9fl oz) of water in a small pan over a medium heat. Increase the heat and bring to the boil, then boil for 5 minutes, or until it turns to a light syrup.

3 Pour the syrup into a shallow, freezerproof non-metallic bowl. Stir in the pared lemon zest and set aside to cool completely.

4 Meanwhile, squeeze the lemons to make about 250ml (9fl oz) of lemon juice. Remove the pared lemon zest strips from the mixture. Stir in the lemon juice and grated zest.

5 Transfer to the freezer for 1–2 hours, or until frozen around the edges and still slightly slushy in the middle. Every 30 minutes or so, use a fork to break up the frozen granita. Continue for 4 hours, or until the mixture has the texture of shaved ice, then leave the granita in the freezer until ready to serve. (See step-by-step technique on p5.)

serves 4

prep 5–10 mins, plus cooling and freezing • cook 5 mins

allow at least 4 hrs for freezing

shallow, freezerproof non-metallic bowl

freeze for up to 1 month

Vanilla ice cream

Nothing beats creamy home-made vanilla ice cream – you'll keep coming back for more.

INGREDIENTS
1 vanilla pod
300ml (10fl oz) milk
3 egg yolks
85g (3 oz) caster sugar
300ml (10fl oz) double cream

METHOD

1 Split the vanilla pod, scrape out the seeds, and put the seeds, vanilla pod, and milk into a heavy saucepan and bring almost to the boil. Remove from the heat, cover, and set aside for 30 minutes.

2 Beat the egg yolks and sugar in a large bowl. Stir in the infused milk then strain back into the pan. Cook the mixture over a low heat, stirring constantly, until the mixture thickens slightly and just coats the back of a spoon. Do not boil the mixture or the custard will curdle. Pour the mixture back into the bowl and cool completely.

3 Whisk the cream into the cooled custard. To freeze the ice cream by hand, pour the mixture into a freezerproof container and freeze for at least 3–4 hours, then whisk to break up any ice crystals. Freeze for a further 2 hours and repeat the process, then freeze until ready to use. To freeze using an ice cream machine, pour the mixture into the prepared freezer bowl and churn according to the manufacturer's instructions. This should take 20–30 minutes. Transfer to a freezerproof container and freeze until needed.

4 To serve the ice cream, remove it from the freezer 20–30 minutes prior to scooping.

serves 4

prep 25 mins, plus freezing • cook 12 mins

allow at least 6 hrs for freezing

ice cream machine desirable • freezerproof container

freeze for up to 3 months

Eton mess

Culinary legend maintains that this medley was concocted after a schoolboy dropped a picnic hamper.

INGREDIENTS

350g (12 oz) ripe strawberries, sliced

2 tbsp caster sugar

2 tbsp orange juice or orange-flavoured
  liqueur

300ml (10fl oz) double cream

125g (4½ oz) ready-baked meringue
  nests

METHOD

1 Put the strawberries in a bowl, sprinkle the sugar over, add the orange juice, then use a fork to crush the mixture.

2 Whip the cream until stiff peaks begin to form. Crush the meringue nests into small pieces.

3 Stir the meringue into the whipped cream. Top with the berries and the juices, and stir together. Serve immediately.

serves 4

prep 10 mins

Strawberry ice cream

Rich and creamy, this strawberry ice cream is enhanced with the tropical flavours of coconut, rum, and lime.

INGREDIENTS

400ml can coconut milk
200g (7 oz) white chocolate, chopped
150g (5½ oz) strawberries, hulled
4 tbsp icing sugar
300ml (10fl oz) double cream
2 tbsp white rum
finely grated zest and juice of 1 lime
lime wedges, to serve
strawberry halves, to serve

METHOD

1 Place the coconut milk and chopped white chocolate into a small saucepan, and heat gently, stirring occasionally, until the chocolate has melted. Set aside and leave to cool slightly.

2 Place the strawberries and icing sugar into a food processor and blend to a purée. Whip the cream to soft peaks, and fold into the coconut mixture along with the strawberry purée, white rum, and lime zest and juice.

3 Pour into a freezerproof container and freeze for 5–6 hours, breaking up the mixture with a fork every 30 minutes, or until firm. Scoop into balls, and serve with lime wedges and strawberry halves.

serves 4

prep 15 mins, plus freezing

allow 5–6 hrs for freezing

food processor
• freezerproof container

after the initial freezing, freeze in an airtight container for up to 3 months

Knickerbocker glory

A childhood favourite, with ice cream, fruit, cream, and sauce. It is traditionally served layered in tall glasses.

INGREDIENTS

2 peaches
8 tbsp strawberry ice cream sauce
8 small scoops strawberry ice cream
4 small scoops chocolate ice cream
150ml (5fl oz) double cream, whipped
1 tbsp sugar strands or sugar balls
4 maraschino cherries
wafer biscuits, to serve

METHOD

1 Place the peaches in a pan of boiling water for 30 seconds to loosen the skins. Drain and halve the fruit, discarding the stones, then peel. Cut the flesh into wedges and place a few into the base of 4 tall glasses or sundae dishes. Top with a scoop of strawberry ice cream and a drizzle of strawberry sauce.
2 Repeat the layering with the remaining peach slices, strawberry ice cream, and strawberry sauce. Place a scoop of chocolate ice cream on top.
3 Place a spoonful of whipped cream to one side of the chocolate ice cream and sprinkle with sugar strands. Decorate with a maraschino cherry and serve each with wafer biscuits.

serves 4

prep 15 mins

Mango sorbet

Juicy, fragrant mangoes make this sorbet a refreshing finish to a summer meal.

INGREDIENTS

2 large mangoes
200g (7 oz) caster sugar
juice of 1 lemon
1 egg white

METHOD

1 Cut the mangoes away from each side of their stones. Discard the stones. Make evenly spaced criss-cross cuts into the flesh of the mango halves, then bend each half backwards to separate out the cubes. Cut the flesh from the skin.

2 Place the mango flesh in a food processor and process until smooth. Press through a sieve and chill until ready to use.

3 Pour 300ml (10fl oz) of water into a saucepan, add the sugar, and heat gently, stirring occasionally. When the sugar has dissolved completely, increase the heat a little and bring to the boil, stirring. Boil for 1 minute, then set aside, and allow to cool completely.

4 Stir the sugar syrup into the mango purée, then stir in the lemon juice. Whisk the egg whites until soft peaks form, then gently fold into the mango mixture.

5 Pour the mixture into a freezerproof container and freeze for at least 4 hours, or until slushy. Mash with a fork to break up any ice crystals. Return to the freezer until solid. (See step-by-step technique on p6.) Alternatively, pour the mixture into an ice cream machine and churn according to the manufacturer's instructions. Transfer to a freezerproof container and freeze until ready to use.

6 Transfer the sorbet to the refrigerator for 15–30 minutes before serving. Scoop into serving dishes and serve.

serves 4

prep 15 mins, plus freezing • cook 10 mins

allow at least 4 hrs for freezing

ice cream machine desirable • food processor • freezerproof container

freeze for up to 3 months

London, New York, Melbourne, Munich, and Delhi

Senior Editor Cécile Landau

Editorial Assistant Shashwati Tia Sarkar

Designer Elma Aquino

Jacket Designer Mark Penfound

DTP Designer Kavita Varma

DK INDIA

Editorial Consultant Dipali Singh

Designer Neha Ahuja

DTP Designer Tarun Sharma

DTP Coordinator Sunil Sharma

Head of Publishing Aparna Sharma

This edition published in 2013
First published in Great Britain in 2012
Material in this publication was previously published
in *The Cooking Book* (2008) and *Cook Express* (2009)
by Dorling Kindersley Limited
80 Strand, London WC2R 0RL
Penguin Group (UK)

Copyright © 2008, 2009, 2012, 2013 Dorling Kindersley
Text copyright © 2008, 2009, 2012 Dorling Kindersley

10 9 8 7 6 5 4 3 2 1
001–192529–Feb/13

ISBN 978-1-4093-2593-2

Printed and bound in China by Hung Hing Printing Co. Ltd.